D1500451

THE CONDITION OF SCULPTURE

A selection of recent sculpture by younger
British and foreign artists

Work by:

Carl Andre	Paul Neagu
Roger Bates	Emma Park
Larry Bell	Nicholas Pope
Michael Bolus	Peter Reginato
Garth Evans	Ulrich Rückriem
David Evison	Lucas Samaras
André Fauteux	Tim Scott
Lloyd Gibson	David Seaton
Katherine Gili	Richard Serra
Nigel Hall	Anthony Smart
Brower Hatcher	Michael Steiner
Julian Hawkes	Sylvia Stone
Peter Hide	Mark di Suvero
Robert Hudson	Brian Thompson
Phillip King	William Tucker
Jeff Lowe	David van de Kop
Loren Madsen	Roger Williams
John Maine	Christopher Wilmarth
Robert Murray	Jacqueline Winsor
David Nash	Isaac Witkin
	James Wolfe

Hayward Gallery London   29 May–13 July 1975

THE CONDITION OF SCULPTURE

A selection of recent sculpture by younger
British and foreign artists

Arts Council of Great Britain 1975

Contents

© Arts Council of Great Britain 1975
Exhibition Officer : Catherine Lampert
Catalogue designed by Roger Huggett/Sinc
Printed in the Netherlands by de Lange/van Leer, Deventer

Soft cover ISBN 0 7287 0054 9
Hard cover ISBN 0 7287 0055 7

Preface

The decision to invite William Tucker to form this exhibition of contemporary sculpture has some history behind it. He had previously proposed what he described as an 'exhibition/congress/convention', to bring to London from Europe and America the best modern sculptors and representative examples of their work. Limitations of time and money made this ambitious scheme unrealizable but the exhibition idea survived and discussion brought into focus the perennial problem of selection.

Various means of dispersing responsibility for selection were considered, but in the end we opted for personal and, in a positive sense, opinionated selection made by a professional sculptor, and we thank Mr. Tucker warmly for the effort and attention he has given to it. The introduction that follows sets out clearly the principles on which he based his choice of work. We have encouraged him to hold fast to the instincts and considerations that have guided his judgement, and also to his underlying desire to assert the continuing vitality of sculpture itself as distinct from the various modes – land art, performance art, conceptual art, etc. – often seen as extensions of it.

Time, money and very particularly space, have prescribed his freedom. Otherwise the exhibition embodies Mr. Tucker's intentions exactly: no one declined the invitation and no one was struck off the list for reasons, say, of distance. It was the selector's decision to exclude older sculptors. This was partly because of greater public familiarity with their work but principally to put the emphasis not on sculptors, even 'important' sculptors, but on the work itself.

An exhibition representing a point of view is easily attacked by those who do not share it and this one no doubt will be. This would only matter if it kept away people who would otherwise be interested in it. We respect William Tucker's views, if they are partisan, their partiality is founded on serious reflection about the nature and history of sculpture evident both in his own work and in his writing. Above all, we believe that, when the cluster of activities we call art is expanding at a dizzying rate, a re-examination and public testing of principles is essential.

We should like to thank the many artists and other lenders who have contributed to this exhibition. We are also indebted to the many people, here and abroad, who drew our attention to sculptors to be considered for selection and supplied us with information where we needed it.

Robin Campbell
Director of Art

Joanna Drew
Director of Exhibitions

Introduction

by William Tucker

This is an exhibition of sculpture, not of sculptors. Nor is the exhibition either polemic or programmatic in intent. My aim was simply to bring together work done in the last two or three years by artists who appear consciously or intuitively to accept the condition of sculpture as I understand it: and who, instead of regarding the physicality and visibility of sculpture as an inhibition, rather take it as a challenge, and a natural and necessary one. Sculpture is the language of the physical[1]: and as with any living language, new thought finds form by stretching the medium itself, not by learning an alien language, or by attempting to invent a wholly new one.

I don't consider it my business here to make claims for the work I have chosen or indeed to describe it in particular. The sculpture is its own evidence; it needs neither apology nor justification, nor the support of great reputations, nor acquaintance with a body of critical literature. If this exhibition is 'about' anything, it is about the persistence of sculpture in face of avant-garde theory and the lack (in this country at least) of serious economic support. The work embraces its homelessness both in the conventional accounts of modernism and in the traditional sculptor's world of public and architectural commissions. Moreover the sculpture in this exhibition represents a fraction only of the younger artists who have continued to make, or who have started making sculpture in recent years. I would say that the number of sculptors separately and independently established in studios and workshops in London alone has never been greater than now. The continuing presence of a wide range of sculpture as a direct physical and visual fact is thus undeniable, though largely unacknowledged. One purpose of the exhibition is to bear witness to this fact. If a hopeful message is carried by the work here, it is that the need to make sculpture 'real' and substantial is a good deal more deeply rooted than critical directive or commercial convenience can dictate.

The world can evidently do without sculpture: sculpture cannot do without the world. Sculpture's *condition* has thus a double sense, deriving from this paradox – the condition or state of the art, its present health (or pathology, if you take that view), the degree to which sculpture seems capable of enforcing its right to exist in our culture: this is the immediate and superficial sense of the phrase. And the condition of sculpture in this first sense will depend at any given moment on the intuitive recognition by sculptors of sculpture's necessary relation with the world, its condition in the broader sense, how sculpture *is* in the world, what are the fundamentally limiting factors. It is by attending to these fundamental limits, and not through evading or escaping them, that sculpture will be seen to advance and prosper. The condition holds not merely for our time and place, but for any time and place.

Sculpture is subject to gravity and revealed by light. Here is the primary condition. Gravity governs sculpture's existence in itself, light discloses sculpture to us. Sculpture's constancy, in time and in space, springs from its fundamental availability to perception. That is, sculpture, however extended, must have a physical boundary: its effect on perception must in the last reckoning derive from the knowledge that the sculpture is not the world, but is a part of it, even if from a certain aspect no boundary is visible. Equally sculpture's effect on perception rests on the knowledge that the boundary is stable: or at least has a sufficient ground of stability that the work's given character is not negated by its own movement exceeding the spectator's conceptual grasp.

These are the fundamental considerations. They precede considerations of image and material, scale and structure and proportion. For most of its history, sculpture has manifested itself in the form of human or animal imagery; but the image is not primary: it is through the rendering of the human form and of drapery, for example, that we are made aware of the underlying condition of gravity: through the figure's known frontality and symmetry, the familiar loci of expression, that the sculpture becomes more visible than other things, other aspects of the world equally revealed by a common light. Again, sculpture's very existence demands that it is made of *some* material, as *some* form is necessitated by its boundedness; but just as the image manifests gravity, so worked-on material manifests the control and modulation of light. Light is the external condition, the given, though of course inconstant: thus sculpture so-called, which depends on a constant and artificial source of light, whether in the environment or in the work itself, offends against this condition: the property of actively *giving* light must remain that of the world, not of sculpture, just as movement is the prerogative of the spectator. For the work to take possession of light and movement, to assume the active role, is ultimately to sacrifice its visibility and so its freedom. When we speak of sculpture as 'active' we do so metaphorically: at most it resists our gaze, receives light, withstands gravity.

7

The 'free-standing' of sculpture must be understood in the light of these primary conditions. *'Free'*, as wholly exposed to our perception, in light; *'standing'*, as withstanding the pull of the earth. We perhaps take the free-standing of sculpture too much for granted, not realizing how recently it was regained for us (by Rodin and Degas), how infrequently it has obtained within the European tradition, and how it is a quality that has to be recovered in each sculpture as it is made even, or especially, now.

Because they coincide in time, the rise of modernism in the visual arts, and the idea of the free-standing in sculpture might be thought to run a common path. The reverse is true, they are totally inimical. Modernism, born and nurtured in painting, generates its deepest energy from the idea of *the plane*. From such a view, the free-standing of sculpture is an intolerable anomaly. Thus Worringer, in the classic statement of early modern criticism, *Abstraction and Empathy*: 'It is relatively simple to wrest the things of the outer world from the flux of happening and to render them perceptible *per se* in their material individuality and closed unity by projecting them on to a plane surface; but the means of sculpture in the round are ill-adapted to this aim, for in truth a free-sculptural representation occupies just as lost and arbitrary a position in the world-picture as its natural model, which the artist had simply tried to eternalize in stone.'[2]

The pressure on sculpture to adopt the painting-directed role of relief has been enormous throughout the modern period, whether the ground of relief has been the wall or the floor, or recently the surface of landscape itself. In each case the condition of gravity is ignored, and sculpture is reduced to a more available, more 'present', but in fact hollow and perverse surrogate-painting. (Only David Smith of the great modern sculptors accepted painting's planar directive and turned it to sculpture's profound advantage, giving sculpture a new order of depth and transparency.)

Sculpture's 'free-standing' is thus more than a neutral description: it is an aspiration. To stand free, for sculpture, demands a positive acceptance and understanding of its condition; and it follows that a free sculpture will remain inconvenient, obtrusive – a challenge to facile and conventional views of history and aesthetic.

Notes

1   To paraphrase Rilke, 'the language of this art was the body . . .',
R. M. Rilke, *The Rodin Book*, *First Part* (1903) from *Selected Works*,
Vol. 1, London, 1967.

2   Wilhelm Worringer, *Abstraction and Empathy* (1908), London, 1948.

Measurements are in metres: height × width × depth.
The illustrations are a selection of recent work by each
artist. The works in the exhibition are marked thus ■.

'35 Blocks and Stones'
Portland Regulus, Portland, Oregon 1973
New York 1974
Blocks, stones 7·70m × 5·24m
Gian Enzo Sperone, N.Y.

a

Carl Andre Born in 1935, Quincy, Massachusetts

Corduroy Road 1973 Corroded sheet metal 3·58m×1·09m

Work for Hayward Gallery, May, 1975

a

Trestle 1974/75 Fibreglass Owned by the artist

b

Trestle 1974/75 Wood, fibreglass ·76m × 1·06m × ·61m Owned by the artist

Roger Bates Born in 1947, London

c

Trestle 4 1974/75 Second view

d

■   **Trestle 4** 1974/75 Wood, fibreglass ·76m×1·06m×·61m Owned by the artist

Trestle 4 1974
Wood, fibreglass ·76m × 1·06m × ·61m
Owned by the artist

2

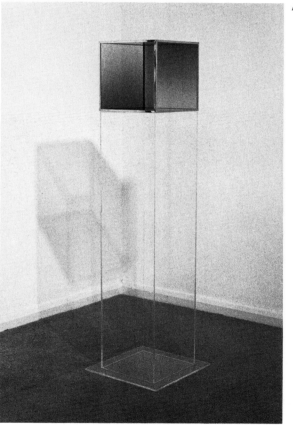

Glass panel 1971/72 Glass 2·44m×1·52m

Cube 1968/69 Glass ·30m× ·30m× ·30m

Larry Bell Born in 1939, Chicago, Illinois

Glass panel 1971/72 Glass 2·13m × 1·22m

Untitled Coated Glass 2 Panels 1971/72
Coated glass 1·83m × 1·83m each panel
Felicity Samuel Gallery

3

Untitled Sculpture No. 2 1974
Painted steel
Owned by the artist

a

Michael Bolus Born in 1934, Cape Town

b

Untitled Sculpture No. 3 1974
Painted steel 2·09m × 3·09m × 2·90m
Owned by the artist, courtesy of Waddington Galleries

4

a

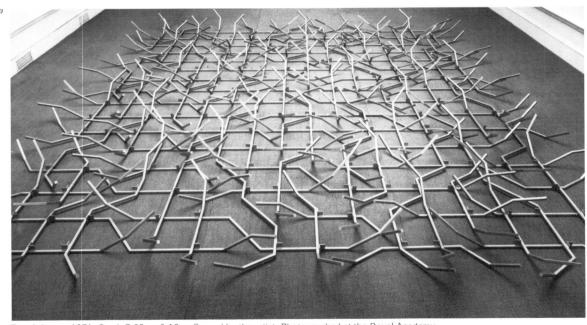

Breakdown 1971 Steel 7·62m × 6·10m Owned by the artist Photographed at the Royal Academy

Garth Evans Born in 1934, Cheshire

b

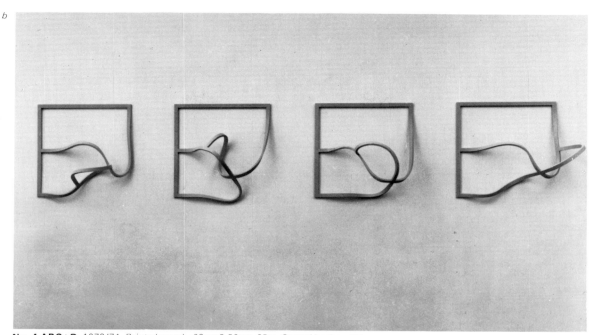

No. 4 ABC+D 1973/74 Painted wood ·63m × 3·50m × ·35m Owned by the artist

c

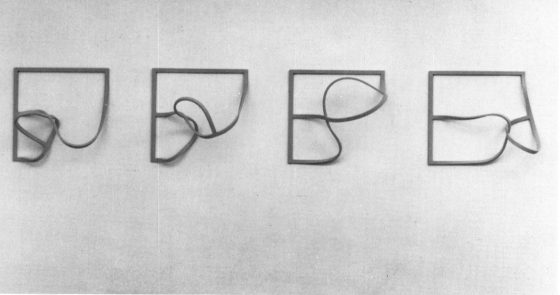

No. 5 ABC+D 1973/74 Painted wood ·63m × 3·50m × ·40m Owned by the artist

Untitled 1975
Plywood ·30m × 2·44m × 2·44m
Owned by the artist

5

a

Number Five 1975 Steel and aluminium 2·18m×3·25m×4·19m Owned by the artist

David Evison Born in 1944, China

b

■ **Number Six** 1975 Steel and aluminium 2·23m × 4·19m × 3·25m Owned by the artist

Number Six 1975
Steel and aluminium 2·23m × 4·19m × 3·25m
Owned by the artist

6

a

■ **Both Ways Now** 1974 Steel 1·57m × 2·18m × 1·14m Owned by the artist

b

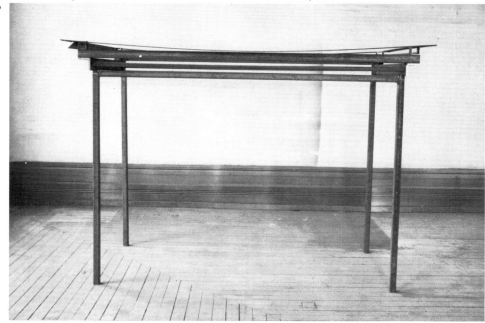

Both Ways Now 1974 Second view

André Fauteux Born in Dunnville, Canada

c

Blacksmith 1974 Steel 1·55m × 4·88m × 1·19m Owned by the artist

d

Nite Watch 1974 Steel 2m × 1·27m × ·73m Owned by the artist

Both Ways Now 1974
Steel 1·57m × 2·18m × 1·14m
Owned by the artist

7

Drawing 1974
Acetate, cord, ink, pencil, shoe-polish
·66m × ·45m
Owned by the artist

a

The Rest is Lies 1974 *detail*
Tubing, cord, canvas, paint, varnish
2·59m × 4·11m × ·15m
Owned by the artist

b

Lloyd Gibson Born 1945, Cambridge

24

c

■ **The Day But One** 1973/74 Canvas, wood, steel, cord, paint, varnish 3·05m × 9·15m × 2·13m Owned by the artist

d

The Day But One 1973/74 Second view

The Day But One 1973/74
Canvas, wood, steel, cord, paint, varnish 3·05m × 9·15m × 2·13m
Owned by the artist

8

a

Shift 1974 Mild steel 1·64m × 1·25m × ·46m Owned by the artist

Katherine Gili Born in 1948, Oxford

■ **Kinchin** December 1974 Mild steel, painted 1·69m × ·97m × 1·01m Owned by the artist

Kinchin December 1974
Mild steel, painted 1·69m × ·97m × 1·01m
Owned by the artist

9

a 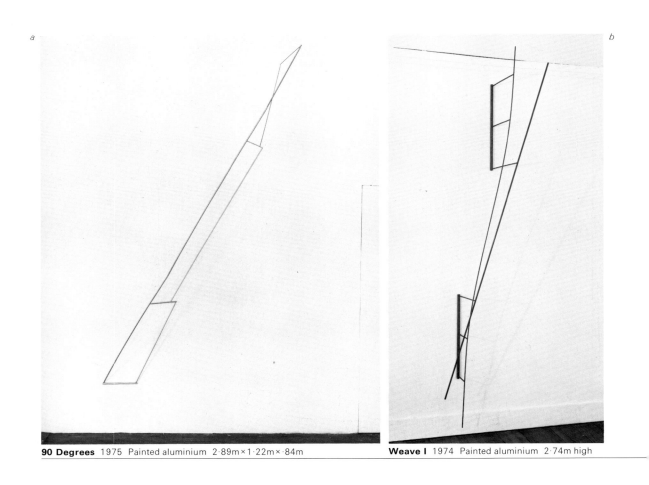 b

90 Degrees 1975 Painted aluminium 2·89m × 1·22m × ·84m   **Weave I** 1974 Painted aluminium 2·74m high

Nigel Hall Born in 1943, Bristol

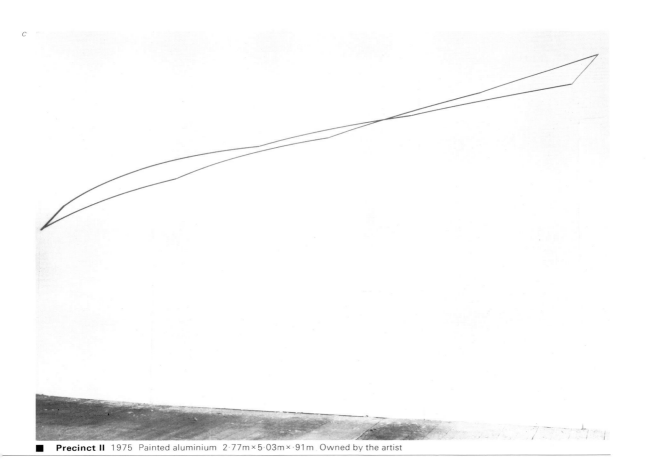

■ **Precinct II** 1975 Painted aluminium 2·77m × 5·03m × ·91m Owned by the artist

Precinct II 1975
Painted aluminium 2·77m × 5·03m × ·91m
Owned by the artist

10

a

Aureola 1975 Steel 1·78m×3·66m×1·60m Owned by the artist, courtesy of André Emmerich Gallery

Brower Hatcher Born in 1942, Atlanta, Georgia

b

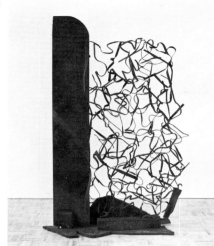

Forecaster 1974
Steel
1·90m × 1·27m × 38m
Owned by the artist

c

Pulsar 1974 Steel 1·52m × 2·59m × 1·47m Owned by the artist

Aureola II 1975
Painted vinyl steel 1·83m × 2·44m × ·91m
Owned by the artist, courtesy of André Emmerich Gallery

11

a

Kami 1973 Leather, wood, steel ·61m × 3·05m × 3·05m Owned by the artist

b

Dawn 1974/75 Wood, steel, paper ·94m × 2·13m × ·45m Owned by the artist

Julian Hawkes Born in 1944, Gloucestershire

c

Source 1974 Wood, rubber ·61m×2·13m×2·98m Owned by the artist

d

Cloud Stone 1974 Paper, stone, steel ·35m×1·39m×1·39m Owned by the artist

Kami 1973
Leather, wood, steel ·61m × 3·05m × 3·05m
Owned by the artist

12

Broadside Spring–Summer 1974
Mild steel, welded and painted
·61m × 1·51m × ·99m
Owned by the artist

a

Shaft Spring 1974
Mild steel, bolted and painted
1·69m × 2·40m × 2·40m
Owned by the artist

b

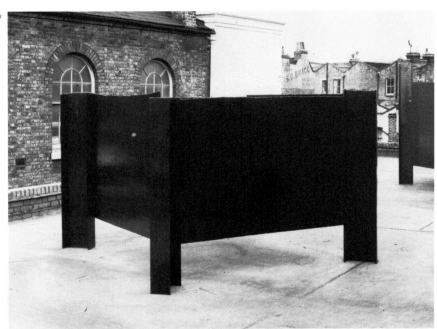

Peter Hide Born in 1944, Surrey

c

Fastback Spring–Summer 1974
Mild steel, welded and painted
·46m × 1·01m × ·62m
Owned by the artist

d

Advance Summer 1974
Mild steel, bolted and painted
3·36m × 2·80m × 1·53m
Owned by the artist

Pomeroy Spring 1975
Mild steel, varnished 1·85m × 2·25m × 3·35m
Owned by the artist

13

Ceramic No. 61 1974
Hand painted porcelain
·245m × ·230m × ·196m

a

Ceramic No. 64 1974
Hand painted porcelain
·286m × ·302m × ·204m

b

Robert Hudson Born in 1938, Salt Lake City, Utah

c

■ **Medicine Ball** 1973 Mixed media ·61m diameter Courtesy of the Hansen Fuller Gallery

Medicine Ball 1973
Mixed media ·61m diameter
Courtesy of the Hansen Fuller Gallery

14

a

■ **Open (Red–Blue) Bound** 1974 Steel 2·13m × 3·66m × 3·66m Rowan Gallery, London

b

Open (Red–Blue) Bound 1974 Second view

Phillip King Born in 1934, Tunis

c

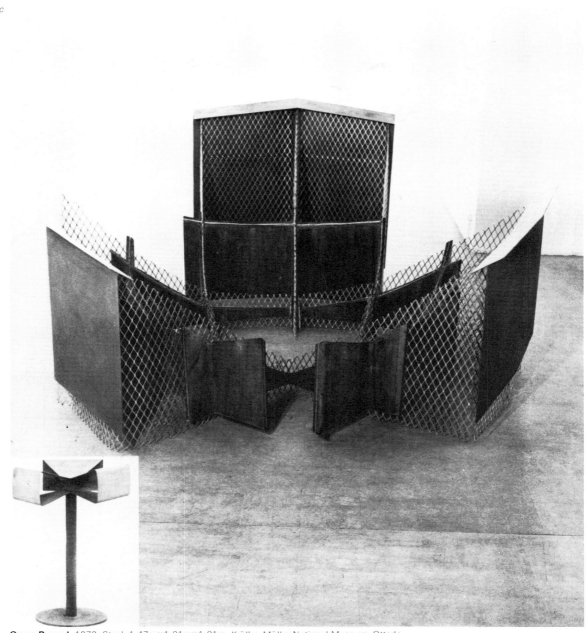

Open Bound 1973 Steel 1·47m×1·01m×1·01m Kröller-Müller National Museum, Otterlo

Open (Red-Blue) Bound 1974
Steel 2·13m × 3·66m × 3·66m
Rowan Gallery, London

15

Wall September 1974
Steel 1·98m×4·27m×·41m
Owned by the artist

a

Wall June 1973
Steel 1·98m×6·1m×·76m
Owned by the artist

b

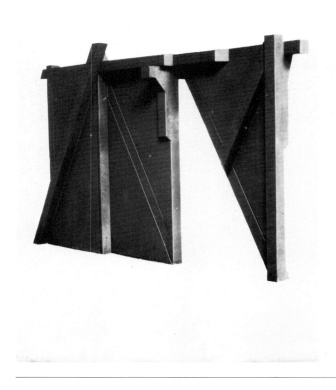

Jeff Lowe Born in 1952, Leigh, Lancashire

C

■ **Sculpture** November 1975 Welded steel 3·05m × 5·49m × 1·22m Owned by the artist

Sculpture November 1975
Welded steel 3·05m × 5·49m × 1·22m
Owned by the artist

16

Leaning Wall February 1975
Norman brick, ss wire
3·66m × 8·84m × 4·57m
Owned by the artist

a

■
Sloped Ring 1974
Redwood blocks, cable, hardware
·61m × 3·96m diameter
Owned by the artist

b

Bricks and Steel Rods
1974 Bricks, steel rods
·91m × 3·05m × 1·06m
Owned by the artist
Photographed at the Los
Angeles County Museum of
Art

c

Loren Madsen   Born in 1943 in Oakland, California

d

Brick and Rod Piece
February 1973
Firebrick, steel rod
4·88m × ·96m × ·61m
Shown at Riko Muzuno
Gallery, Los Angeles

Sloped Ring 1974
Redwood blocks, cable, hardware ·61m × 3·96m diameter
Owned by the artist

17

a

Untitled 1973/74 Limestone ·23m×·25m×·25m Owned by the artist

John Maine Born in 1942, Bristol

44

b

Untitled 1974 Limestone ·23m × ·23m × ·22m Owned by the artist

Untitled 1975
Portland Whitbed maximum dimension 1·01m
Owned by the artist

18

Cumbria 1966/67 Corten steel, painted yellow 4·57m × 9·15m × 4·57m Now at Vancouver International Airport

b

Nordkyn 1974 Corten steel, painted blue Wayne State University, Detroit

Robert Murray Born in 1936, Vancouver, Canada

c

Agulapak 1974
Aluminium, painted light green
1·87m × 1·95m × 1·67m
Owned by the artist,
Courtesy of Paula Cooper Gallery

d

Togiak 1974
Aluminium, painted green
2·13m × 1·93m × 1·85m
Owned by the artist,
Courtesy of Paula Cooper Gallery

Agulapak 1974
Aluminium, painted light green 1·87m × 1·95m × 1·67m
Owned by the artist, courtesy of Paula Cooper Gallery

19

a

In the Table 1974 Wood 1·37m×1·06m×1·06m Owned by the artist

David Nash Born in 1945, Surrey

b

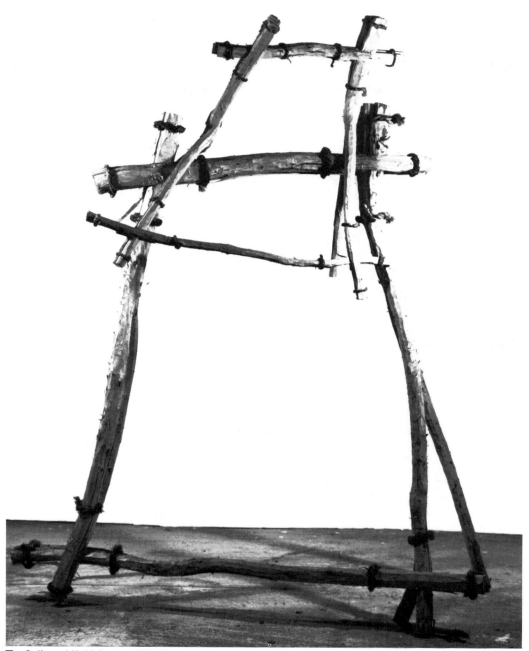

■ **Split and Held Across** 1972 Wood and rope 2·13m × 1·83m × ·76m Owned by the artist

Split and Held Across 1972
Wood 2·13m × 1·83m × ·76m
Owned by the artist

20

a

Inquest, Tools 1970/74 Mixed media Photo-documentation: Generative Art Group

b

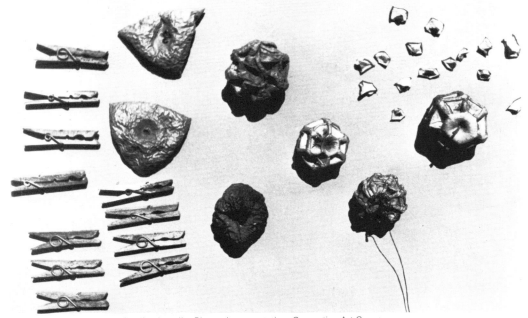

Apple, Event, Bites 1973 Mixed media Photo-documentation: Generative Art Group

Paul Neagu   Born in 1938, Bucharest, Rumania

c

■
Object Tactile, 30 Cells:
three cells containing small objects 1971/72
Wood, leather, gesso
·20m × ·36m × ·14m
Owned by the artist

d

Object Tactile, 30 Cells 1971/72 Second view

Object Tactile, 30 Cells 1971/72
Wood, leather, gesso ·20m × ·36m × ·14m
Owned by the artist

21

4 Diagonals 1974
Wood ·99m, ·76m, ·53m, ·30m, ·7m
Owned by the artist

a

b

4 Diagonals 1974 Wood ·99m, ·76m, ·53m, ·30m, ·7m

Emma Park   Born in 1950, Leeds

52

c

4 Diagonals 1974 Second view

d

■ **Single Diagonal** 1974 Wood ·99m × 1·22m × ·23m Owned by the artist

Single Diagonal February 1974
Wood ·99m × 1·22m × ·23m
Owned by the artist

22

Elm Wood Column 1974
Wood 2·28m high
Owned by the artist

Oak Wood Column 1973
Wood 1·52m high
Owned by the artist

Walnut Wood Column 1974
Wood 2·13m high
Owned by the artist

a   b   c

Nicholas Pope   Born in 1949, Sydney, Australia

d

The Arch Spring—Summer 1974 Oak wood blocks 3·05m radius Owned by the artist

Oak Wood Column 1973
Wood 1·52m high
Owned by the artist

23

Mix and Mingle 1973
Steel ·91m × ·89m × ·56m
Lent by the Chase Manhattan Bank
Art Collection

a

b

Air 1975 Painted steel 1·52m × 1·67m × 2·44m Owned by the artist

Peter Reginato Born in 1945, Dallas, Texas

56

c

Hannibal 1972 Steel 3·35m×2·44m×·96m Collection of Storm King Art Center

Mix and Mingle 1973
Steel ·91m × ·89m × ·56m
Lent by the Chase Manhattan Bank Art Collection

24

Bluestone of Aachen 1969
Sawn (stone circular saw)
1·40m × ·60m × 1·15m
Collection Renker, Düren

Dolomite Stone 1973
Cut (stone circular saw)
2·20m × 1·10m × ·67m
Owned by the artist

a

b

Ulrich Rückriem   Born 1938, Düsseldorf

Belgian Granite 1974
Cleft
·86m × 1m × 1m
Owned by the artist

Dolomite Stone 1970
Cleft (hammer)
·12m × 1m × 1m
Collection of Hock, Krefeld

Belgian Granite 1969
Cleft (hammer and chisel)
·3m × 1.20m × 2m
Kaiser Wilhelm Museum, Krefeld

Dolomite Stone 1968
Cleft (hammer and iron wedge)
·95m × ·42m × ·42m
Kaiser Wilhelm Museum, Krefeld

c

d

e

f

Four Plates Granite
Belgian Granite ·10m × 2·5m × 1·5m
Owned by the artist

25

Untitled Book No. 4 1962
Mixed media
Collection of the Museum of Modern Art, N.Y.

Box No. 10 1963
Mixed media · 18m × ·35m × ·28m
Collection of Adam Aronson

Chair Transformation No. 5 1969/70
Wire mesh ·91m × ·68m × ·45m
Pace Gallery, N.Y.

Photo Transformation 1973
Polaroid ·7m × ·7m
Collection of Fogg Art Museum, Cambridge, Mass.

a

b

c

d

Lucas Samaras Born in 1936, Kastoria, Greece

e

■ **Stiff Box No. 12** 1971 Corten steel 1·92m×1·39m×·35m Collection of Mr & Mrs Wilfred P. Cohen

Stiff Box No. 12 1971
Corten steel 1·92m × 1·39m × ·35m
Collection of Mr & Mrs Wilfred P. Cohen

26

a

Cathedral 1970/71

b

Bird in Arras III 1968 Courtesy Museum of Fine Arts, Boston

Tim Scott Born in 1937, London

62

c

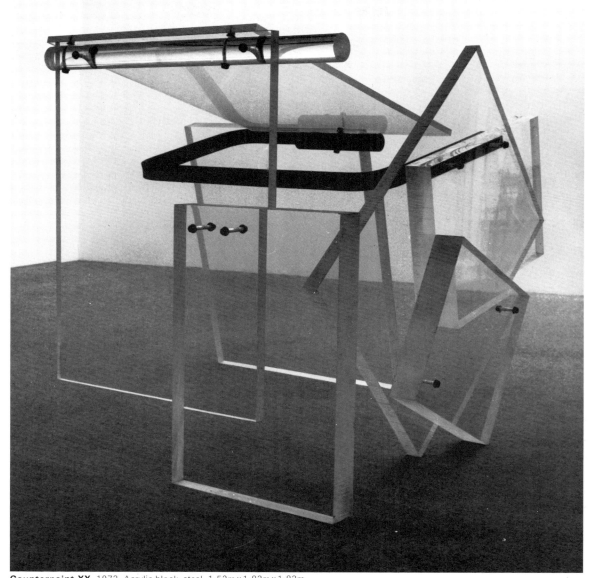

Counterpoint XX 1973 Acrylic block, steel 1·52m × 1·83m × 1·83m

Counterpoint XXI 1974
Acrylic block, forged steel 1·83m × 1·52m × 1·83m
Waddington Galleries

27

a

Maquette 1974 Steel ·61m × ·30m × ·30m Owned by the artist

b

Axis I 1974 Steel 2·44m × 2·44m × ·91m Owned by the artist

David Seaton Born in 1943, England

c

■ **Ithaca I** 1974 Steel 2·44m × 1·22m × 1·22m Owned by the artist

d

Ithaca II 1975 Steel 2·74m × 2·74m × 1·52m Owned by the artist

Ithaca I 1974
Steel 2·44m × 1·22m × 1·22m
Owned by the artist

28

a

Stepped Elevation 1973/74 Hot rolled steel, 12 plates, each 2·44m × 3·66m × ·03m

b

Stepped Elevation 1973/74 Second view

Richard Serra   Born in 1939, San Francisco

c

Equal Parallel and Right-Angle Elevation 1973 Hot rolled steel 2 pieces: 4·50m × ·61m × ·13m 2 pieces: ·68m × ·61m × ·13m

d

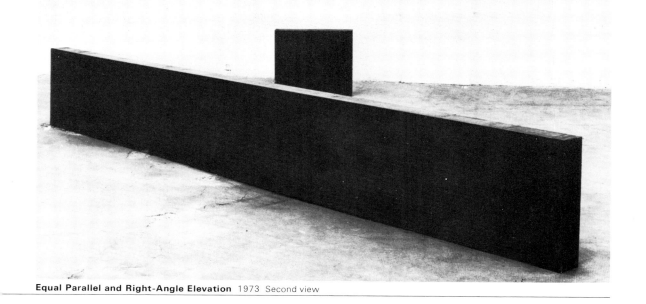

Equal Parallel and Right-Angle Elevation 1973 Second view

Installation for Hayward Gallery 1975

29

a

■ **Brown** 1974 Mild steel 1·43m × 2·80m × 1·52m Owned by the artist

b

Curve 1974 Mild steel 1·16m × 2·20m × 1·28m Owned by the artist

Anthony Smart Born in 1949, Yorkshire

c

Double Curve 1974 Mild steel 1·52m × 2·28m × 1·60m Owned by the artist

d

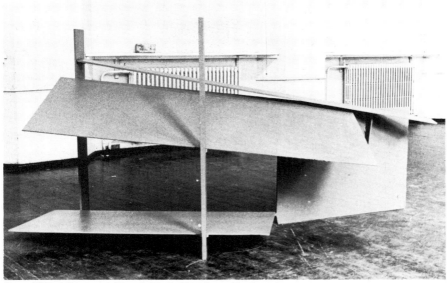

Grey 1975 Mild steel 1·52m × 2·54m × ·40m Owned by the artist

Brown December 1974
Painted mild steel 1·43m × 2·80m × 1·52m
Owned by the artist

30

a

Piece No. 10 1969 Corten steel ·28m × 1·37m × 1·10m Owned by the artist

b

Mana 1972 Corten steel 1·33m × 3·96m × 2·51m Collection of Mr & Mrs Oscar Kolin

Michael Steiner Born in 1945, New York

70

c

Bird 1972 Corten steel 1·37m × 2·44m × 2·44m Collection of Museum of Fine Arts, Boston

d

■ **Knossos** 1972 Corten steel 1·42m × 2·74m × 2·33m Collection of Lois and George de Menil

Knossos 1972
Corten steel 1·42m × 2·74m × 2·33m
Collection of Lois and George de Menil

31

a

Crystal Palace Plexiglass

b

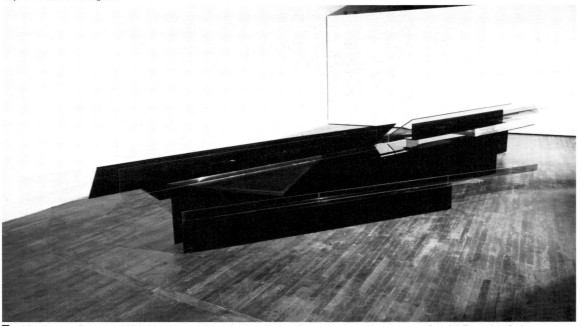

■ **Manhattan Express** 1974 Plexiglass 1·01m × 9·15m × 3·05m Owned by the artist, courtesy of André Emmerich Gallery

Sylvia Stone Born in 1928, Toronto, Canada

c

Manhattan Express 1974 Second view

Manhattan Express 1974
Plexiglass 1·01m × 9·15m × 3·05m
Owned by the artist, courtesy of André Emmerich Gallery

32

a

Etoile Polaire 1973/74 Steel 22·87m×18·30m×18·30m

Mark di Suvero Born in 1933, Shanghai, China

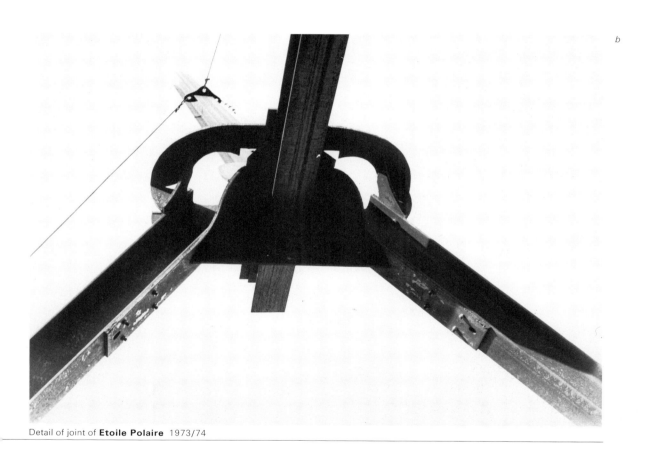

b

Detail of joint of **Etoile Polaire** 1973/74

Untitled 1974
Steel 2·38m × 1·45m
Owned by the artist, courtesy of Richard Bellamy

33

a

Landscape Sculpture 1973 Mild steel, G.R.P. with sand filler 1·80m×1·72m×2·05m Owned by the artist

b

Concrete Sculpture 1974 Mild steel, cement, Portland stone 1·88m×3·60m×1·27m Owned by the artist

Brian Thompson Born in 1950, Morley, Yorkshire

■
Stone Sculpture 1973
Sandstone, mild steel, wood
1·52m × ·61m × ·53m
Owned by the artist

Stone Sculpture 1973 Second view

c

d

Stone Sculpture 1973
Sandstone, mild steel, wood 1·52m × ·61m × ·53m
Owned by the artist

34

a

Tunnel 1960 Iron ·38m × ·71m × ·38m Private Collection

William Tucker Born in 1935, Cairo

78

b

■ **Tunnel** 1972/75 Laminated wood, aluminium 2·13m × 3·84m × 3·27m Owned by the artist

Tunnel 1972/75
Laminated wood, aluminium 2·13m × 3·84m × 3·27m
Owned by the artist

35

a

Sculpture at the Kröller-Müller National Museum, Otterlo 1974 Sand, steel 4·57m long

b

Untitled Sculpture

David van de Kop Born in 1937, The Hague, Holland

c

Sculpture at the Kröller-Müller National Museum, Otterlo 1974

Landscape 1974
Iron, sand 2m × 6m × 6m
Owned by the artist, made at the Hayward Gallery

36

a

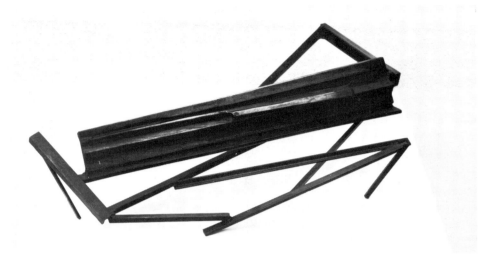

Feather 1973 Steel ·15m×·48m×·35m Collection of Stuart Waltzer

b

Neck Path 1972 Steel 1·29m×2·21m×1·45m Owned by the artist

Roger Williams Born in 1943, Dayton, Ohio

c

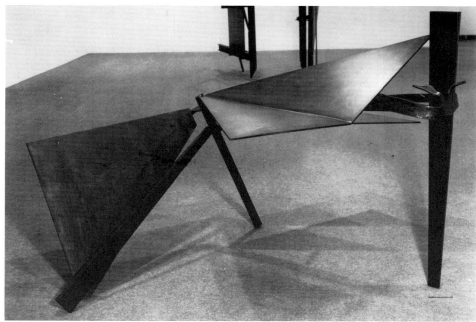

Particular Reel 1974 Steel Owned by the artist

d

■ **So Long** 1972 Steel 1·14m × 2·82m × 1·80m Owned by the artist, courtesy of André Emmerich Gallery

So Long 1972
Steel 1·14m × 2·82m × 1·80m
Owned by the artist, courtesy of André Emmerich Gallery

37

Slip 1972
Steel and glass
·76m × 1·52m × ·28m
Owned by the artist

a

My Divider 1972/73
Steel and glass
1·52m × 2·28m × 2·13m
Owned by the artist

b

Christopher Wilmarth   Born in 1943, Sonoma, California

c

■ **Clearing for a Standing Man No. 4** 1973 Steel and glass 2·03m×1·52m×·12m Owned by the artist

Clearing for a Standing Man No. 4 1973
Steel and glass 2·03m × 1·52m × ·12m
Owned by the artist

38

1″×1″ Piece 1974
Wood, nails
1·14m × 1·14m
Owned by the artist

a

Plywood Square 1973
Plywood and hemp
·61m × 1·17m × 1·17m
Collection of the Australian National Gallery

b

Jacqueline Winsor Born in 1941, Newfoundland, Canada

c

Untitled 1969/70 Hemp ·23m diameter, 3·71m length Owned by the artist

d

■ **Four Corners** 1972 Wood, hemp ·68m × 1·22m × 1·22m Collection of the Allen Memorial Art Museum, Oberlin College

Four Corners 1972
Wood, hemp ·68m × 1·22m × 1·22m
Collection of the Allen Memorial Art Museum, Oberlin College

39

a

Kosazaan 1972 Collection Alfred Kleinbaum, Connecticut

b

Sabras 1973 Collection Mrs P. Nasher, Texas

Isaac Witkin Born in 1936, Johannesburg, South Africa

c

Dingaan 1971/72 Collection Robert Meyerhoff

d

■ **Everglades** 1975 Mild steel 1·08m × 3·05m × 2·92m Collection of Mr and Mrs A. Hunter Land II, San Francisco, California

Everglades 1975
Mild steel 1·08m × 3·05m × 2·92m
Collection of Mr and Mrs A. Hunter Land II, San Francisco, California

40

a

Rill 1973 Steel ·96m×1·80m×4·09m Owned by the artist

James Wolfe Born in 1944, New York City

b

Across and Under 1974 Mild steel 1·06m × 2·56m × 1·45m Private Collection

c

■ **Five Across** 1974 Steel 1·62m × 1·42m × 3·53m Private Collection, London

Five Across 1974
Steel 1·62m × 1·42m × 3·53m
Private Collection, London

41

Biographies

Carl Andre

Born in 1935 in Quincy, Massachusetts. Finished two pieces 'Last Ladder' and 'Pyramid' in 1959. 'Pyramid' first exhibited in 1964. Made 'Lever' in 1966. One-man exhibition at the Solomon R. Guggenheim Museum of Art, N.Y. in 1970. Presently exhibiting with the John Weber Gallery, N.Y.

Roger Bates

Born in 1947 in London. Studied at St Martin's School of Art, 1966–71. Exhibited in 'New Sculpture 1970', toured by the Arts Council. 1971–3, employed as a machinist, salesman, security guard, civil servant. Presently teaching at St Martin's School of Art.

Larry Bell

Born in 1939 in Chicago, Illinois. Moved to California in 1945. Studied at Chouinard Art Institute, Los Angeles, 1957–59. Painted from 1959–61 in Venice, California. Developed into constructionist painting reliefs using glass and canvas. One-man show at Pace Gallery, N.Y., 1965. Began designing and fabricating sculptural projects with own equipment for surface treatment of glass panels, 1967–70. Experimented with sound equipments and psychological aspects of space environments. Travelled through Southeast Asia, Australia and the Far East, 1973. Moved to New Mexico in 1973.

Michael Bolus

Born in 1934 in Cape Town. Studied at St Martin's School of Art, 1959–62. Exhibited at Waddington Galleries, London, 1970, 1971.

Garth Evans

Born in 1934 in Cheshire. Studied at Manchester Regional College of Art and the Slade School of Fine Art, 1955–60.

British Steel Corporation Fellowship, 1969; Visiting Professorship, Minneapolis College of Art & Design, 1973. Presently teaching at Camberwell School of Art and visiting lecturer at St Martin's and the Slade Schools of Art.

One-man exhibitions at the Rowan Gallery, London, 1962–74, Leeds Polytechnic, Ferens Art Gallery, Hull and Sheffield School of Art, 1971. Group exhibitions include: 10th Biennale for Sculpture, Open Air Museum of Sculpture, Middelheim, Antwerp, 1969; 'British Sculpture '72', Royal Academy, London, 1972; Peter Stuyvesant City Sculpture Project, Cardiff, 1972.

David Evison

Born in 1944 in China. Studied at Leeds College of Art and St Martin's School of Art. Living in London.

André Fauteux

Born in Dunnville, Canada. One-man exhibitions: Dunkelman Gallery, Toronto, 1971, 1973; Jared Sable Gallery, Toronto, 1974, 1975. Group exhibitions include: Gallery Ivan Spence, Ibiza, 1968; Salon de Mayo, Barcelona, 1968; Isaacs Gallery, Toronto, 1971. Awarded Canada Council Arts Bursaries 1970–71; 1971–72.

Lloyd Gibson

Born in 1945 in Cambridge. Studied at Newcastle University, 1964–68. Awarded the Hatton Scholarship, the Bunzl Travelling Scholarship and the Annabella Smiles Travelling Scholarship. At present Senior Lecturer in the Fine Art Department, Newcastle upon Tyne Polytechnic.

One-man exhibitions at the Gulbenkian Gallery, Newcastle upon Tyne, 1969 and the D.L.I. Museum, Durham, 1971. Group exhibitions include: 'Aerial Structures', Sunderland Arts Centre, 1973; 'British Sculptors: Attitudes to Drawing', Sunderland Arts Centre and Wolverhampton Art Gallery, 1974; Peter Stuyvesant

Northern Painters and Sculptors
Exhibition (Major Award Winner), 1974.

Katherine Gili

Born in 1948 in Oxford. Studied at Bath
Academy of Art, 1966–70 and St Martin's
School of Art, 1971–73. Presently teaching
at Norwich School of Art and St Martin's
School of Art. Started working at Stockwell
Depot in 1973.

Group exhibitions include: 'Platform '73',
Museum of Modern Art, Oxford, 1973;
'Six Sculptors', Chelsea Gallery,
London, 1974; 'New Sculpture', Stockwell
Depot, 1974; Group show, Norwich
Cathedral Cloisters, 1975.

Nigel Hall

Born in 1943 in Bristol. Studied at the West
of England College of Art, 1960–64; Royal
College of Art, 1964–67. Awarded the
Harkness Fellowship, travelled in U.S.A.,
Canada and Mexico,. 1967–69. One-man
exhibitions at Galerie Givaudan, Paris,
1967; Nicholas Wilder Gallery, Los
Angeles, 1968, 1972, 1975; Galerie
Neuendorf, Hamburg, 1970 and Cologne,
1970; Serpentine Gallery, London, 1970;
Felicity Samuel Gallery, London, 1972,
1974; Primo Piano, Galleria d'Arte, Rome,
1974; Robert Elkon Gallery, N.Y., 1974;
Galleri Galax, Göteborg, 1975.

Group exhibitions include: 'New British
Painting and Sculpture', U.C.L.A. Galleries,
Los Angeles and tour, 1967–69; 'British
Sculpture '72', Royal Academy, London,
1972; Salon des Réalitiés Nouvelles, Paris,
1972; Peter Stuyvesant Sculpture Project,
1972; 'Earth Images', Gallery of Modern
Art, Edinburgh and tour, 1973; Bradford
Print Biennale (Alecto Commission Prize),
1974; 'British Sculptors: Attitudes to
Drawing', Sunderland Arts Centre, 1974;
C.A.S. Art Fair, Mall Galleries, London,
1975; 'British Art, Mid '70s', Jahrhundert-
halle, Hoechst, 1975, International
Exhibition of Graphic Art, Ljublijana, 1975;
'The Sculptor as Draughtsman', JPL
Gallery, London, 1975; 9th Paris Biennale,
Museums of Modern Art, Paris, 1975.

Brower Hatcher

Born in 1942 in Atlanta, Georgia. Studied
at Vanderbilt University, Nashville, Tenn.,
1961–63; Pratt Institute, New York, 1963–67
and St Martin's School of Art, 1969–72.

One-man exhibitions at the Museum of
Modern Art, Oxford, 1971; Kasmin Ltd.,
London, 1972; and the André Emmerich
Gallery, New York, 1973–1975.

Julian Hawkes

Born in 1944 in Gloucestershire. Studied
at the West of England College of Art and
the Slade School of Fine Art. At present
assistant to Phillip King and teaching at
Norwich School of Art.

Peter Hide

Born in 1944 in Surrey. Studied at Croydon
College of Art, 1961–64; St Martin's
School of Art, 1964–67. Teaching trip to
Victoria and Vancouver, Canada in 1974.
Presently teaching at Norwich School of
Art and St Martin's School of Art.

Exhibited at Stockwell Depot, London,
1968–74 and in travelling exhibitions from
Stockwell in Great Britain and Scandinavia.
Sculpture by John Foster and Peter Hide
at Marble Hill House, 1973. Commissioned
to make pieces for the Arts Council, 'New
Sculpture', 1969; Northern Arts
Association, D.L.I. Arts Centre, Durham,
1970; Peter Stuyvesant City Sculpture
Project, 1972.

Robert Hudson

Born in 1938 in Salt Lake City, Utah.
Studied at San Francisco Art Institute.
Awarded a Visual Arts Grant, National
Endowment for the Arts, 1972. Living in
Stinson Beach, California.

One-man exhibitions include: San
Francisco Art Institute, 1965; Nicholas
Wilder Gallery, Los Angeles, 1967; Allen
Frumkin Gallery, New York and Chicago,
1965–1972; Michael Walls Gallery, San
Francisco, 1970; 'The Star Show',
University Art Museum, University of

California, Berkeley, 1972; 'Robert Hudson/Richard Shaw, Work in Porcelain', San Francisco Museum of Art, 1973; Hansen Fuller Gallery, San Francisco, 1975. Included in 'Sculpture of the Sixties', Los Angeles County Museum of Art and the Philadelphia Museum of Art, 1967.

Phillip King

Born in 1934 in Tunis. Read languages at Cambridge University, 1954–57. Studied at St Martin's School of Art, 1957–58. Assistant to Henry Moore, 1958–60. Appointed Trustee of the Tate Gallery. Teaching at St Martin's School of Art.

One-man exhibitions include: Rowan Gallery, London, 1964–75; Whitechapel Art Gallery, London, 1968; European Museum Tour: Kröller-Müller Museum, Otterlo, Holland; Kunsthalle, Düsseldorf; Kunsthalle, Berne; Musée Galiéra, Paris, 1974–75.

Group exhibitions include: 5th Guggenheim International Exhibition, N.Y., 1967; Venice Biennale (with Bridget Riley), 1968; 'Contemporary Art-Dialogue between the East and West', National Museum of Modern Art, Tokoyo, 1969; 'International Sculptors Symposium for Expo '70', Osaka, Japan; 'British Sculpture out of the Sixties', ICA, London, 1972; 'Henry Moore to Gilbert & George – Modern British Art from the Tate Gallery', Palais des Beaux Arts, Brussels, 1973.

Jeff Lowe

Born in 1952 in Leigh, Lancashire. Studied at Leicester Polytechnic, 1970–71. Presently studying at St Martin's School of Art. One-man exhibition at The Leicester Galleries, London, 1974. Group exhibitions include: 'New Contemporaries', Camden Arts Centre, London, 1974; 'Six Sculptors', Chelsea Gallery, London, 1974; 'British Sculptors: Attitudes to Drawing', Sunderland Arts Centre, 1974; Paris Biennale, 1975.

Loren Madsen

Born in 1943 in Oakland, California. Studied at Reed College, Portland, Oregon, 1961–63 and U.C.L.A., 1963–70. One-man exhibitions at Riko Mizuno Gallery, Los Angeles, 1973, 1974; David McKee Gallery, N.Y., 1975; 'Projects', Museum of Modern Art, N.Y., 1975. Group exhibitions include: 'Young Sculptors', Scripps College, Claremont, California, 1972; 'Constructions', L.B.C.C., Long Beach, 1974; 'Los Angeles Six/ Summer '74', Los Angeles County Museum of Art, 1974; '24 from Los Angeles', Los Angeles Municipal Art Gallery, 1974.

John Maine

Born in 1942 in Bristol. Studied at the West of England College of Art, 1960–64 and the Royal College of Art, 1964–67. Awarded Walther Neurath prize, 1966 and Fellowship, Gloucestershire College of Art & Design, 1967–69. Presently teaching at Winchester, Gloucestershire and Kingston Colleges of Art. One-man exhibition at the Serpentine Gallery, London 1972. Group exhibitions include: 'Steel Sculpture', Mappin Art Gallery, Sheffield, 1972; Sculpture at South Hill Park, Bracknell, 1973/74; Bradford Print Biennale, 1974; City Art Project, Portsmouth, 1974.

Robert Murray

Born in 1936 in Vancouver B.C., Canada. Studied at Saskatchewan School of Art 1956–58. One-man exhibitions include: Betty Parsons Gallery, N.Y., 1965, 1966, 1968; David Mirvish Gallery, Toronto 1967, 1968, 1972, 1974; Jewish Museum, N.Y., 1967; Dag Hammarskjold Plaza, N.Y., 1971, 1972; Paula Cooper Gallery, N.Y., 1974.

Group exhibitions include: 'Sculpture of the Sixties', Los Angeles County Museum of Art, 1967; lle Biennale, Middelheim, Antwerp, 1971; Emma Lake Workshop, Norman Mackenzie Art Gallery, Regina, 1973.

David Nash

Born 1945, Surrey. Studied at Brighton Art College and Kingston Art College, 1963–67. Moved to Blaenau Ffestiniog, North Wales, 1967. Chelsea School of Art, Postgraduate year, 1970. Visiting lecturer at Wolverhampton, Newcastle, Norwich and Kingston Colleges of Art. Living in Blaenau Ffestiniog.

Paul Neagu

Born in 1938 in Bucharest, Rumania. Made first objects in 1954. One-man exhibition at Amphora Gallery, Bucharest with tactile objects, 1969. 'Four Rumanian Artists', Richard Demarco Gallery, Edinburgh, 1969. 'Palpable Art Manifesto' and exhibition with palpable environment shown at Edinburgh Festival, 1969. Worked on ceramics in Paris. Exhibited at the Sigi Krauss Gallery, London, 1971. Events performed between 1971–1974 include 'Blind's Bite', 'Apple', 'Waffle Machine', 'Horizontal Rain', 'Going Tornado' and 'Going'. Lecture and demonstration of 'generative art forms' at Queens University Festival, Belfast, 1972. Founder of 'Generative Art Group'. 'Serpentine Sculpture 1973', London. 'Earth Images', Gallery of Modern Art, Edinburgh and tour, 1973. One-man exhibition at the Museum of Modern Art, Oxford, 1975.

Emma Park

Born in 1950 in Leeds. Studied at Chelsea School of Art (painting), 1968–72. Post-graduate student at the Slade School of Fine Art, 1972–74. Allocated one of the studios belonging to the Stedelijk Museum, Amsterdam, February–May 1975. Group exhibitions include: Portsmouth City Art Project, 1974/75; Lucy Milton Gallery, London, 1974.

Nicholas Pope

Born in 1949. Studied at Bath Academy of Art, 1970–73. Group exhibitions at the Festival Gallery, Bath, 1973 and Portsmouth Museum, 1974. Rumanian Government Exchange Scholarship 1974/75. Exhibited at The Garage, London, 1975.

Peter Reginato

Born in 1945 in Dallas, Texas. Studied at the San Francisco Art Institute, 1963–66. Winner of Allen Center National Sculpture Competition for large scale sculpture for Houston, Texas. One-man exhibitions at the Tibor de Nagy Gallery, N.Y., 1971–75. Group exhibitions include: Park Place Invitational, N.Y., 1967; Whitney Museum of American Art, 1970, 1973; 'Richard Brown Baker Collection', Rhode Island School of Design, 1973; Storm King Art Center, N.Y., 1974.

Ulrich Rückriem

Born in 1938 in Düsseldorf. After secondary school was apprenticed to a stonemason. Journeyman at the Dombauhütte, Cologne, 1959. Since 1961 working as a sculptor and living in Mönchengladbach.

One-man exhibitions include: Leopold Hoesch Museum, Düren, 1965; Galerie Ernst, Hannover, 1969, 1971; Konrad Fischer, Düsseldorf, 1969, 1971, 1974; Museum Haus Lange, Krefeld, 1970; Mayfair Gallery, London, 1971; Galerie Paul Maenz, Cologne, 1971, 1974; Kabinett für aktuelle Kunst, Bremerhaven, 1971; Videogalerie Gerry Schum, Düsseldorf, 1971; Paula Cooper Gallery, N.Y., 1972; Kunsthalle, Tübingen, 1973; Stadtisches Museum, Mönchengladbach, 1973; Kunstverein, Frankfurt, 1974.

Published book *Ulrich Rückriem, Skulturen 68–73* (DuMont, Cologne, 1973).

Lucas Samaras

Born in 1936 in Kastoria, Greece. Studied at Rutgers University, 1955–59 and Columbia Graduate School of Art History, 1959–62. Taught at Yale University and Brooklyn College. One-man exhibitions include: Reuben Gallery, N.Y., 1959; Green Gallery, N.Y., 1961, 1964; Pace

Gallery, N.Y., 1966–75, Museum of Contemporary Art, Chicago, 1971; Whitney Museum of American Art, N.Y., 1972 (retrospective with catalogue 'Autobiography, Autointerviews, Auto-polaroids'); 'Pastels', Museum of Modern Art, N.Y., 1975. Articles by the artist include: 'An Exploratory Dissection of Seeing', *Artforum*, December, 1967; 'Greece, 1967: A Reconstituted Diary', *Artforum*, October, 1968; 'Auto-polaroids, 16 pages of autopolaroids by Lucas Samaras', *Art in America*, November–December, 1970. To be published: *Samaras*, by Kim Levin (Harry Abrams).

Tim Scott

Born in 1937 in London. Studied at St Martin's School of Art and at the Architectural Association, London. Worked in Paris in the Le Corbusier-Wogenscky studio, 1959–61.

One-man exhibitions include: Waddington Galleries, London, 1966, 1969, 1971, 1974; Whitechapel Gallery, London, 1967; Museum of Modern Art, Oxford, 1969; Lawrence Rubin Gallery, N.Y., 1969, 1971, 1974; Museum of Fine Arts, Boston and The Corcoran Gallery of Art, Washington, D.C., 1973.

Group exhibitions include: 'The New Generation: 1965', Whitechapel Gallery, London, 1965; 'Primary Structures', Jewish Museum, N.Y., 1966; 'The Alistair McAlpine Gift', Tate Gallery, London, 1971.

David Seaton

Born in 1943, England. Studied at Batley School of Art, 1960–64; Leeds College of Art, 1964–65; St Martin's School of Art, 1973–74. Presently working at Greenwich and teaching at Croydon School of Art. Group exhibitions include: Bradford City Art Gallery, 1967; 'New Contemporaries', Camden Arts Centre, 1974; 'Six Sculptors', Chelsea Gallery, 1974.

Richard Serra

Born in 1939 in San Francisco. Studied at University of California and Yale University. One-man exhibitions include: Galleria La Salita, Rome, 1966; Galerie Ricke, Cologne, 1968, 1973; Leo Castelli, N.Y., 1970, 1974; Pasadena Art Museum, Pasadena, California, 1970; School of Visual Arts, N.Y., 1974. Group exhibitions include: 'Nine at Castelli', Leo Castelli, N.Y., 1968; 'Square Pegs in Round Holes', Stedilijk Museum, Amsterdam, 1969; 'When Attitudes Become Form', Kunsthalle, Bern and ICA, London, 1969; 'Art and Technology', Los Angeles County Museum, 1971; 'Interventions in Land-scapes', Hayden Gallery, M.I.T., Cambridge, Mass., 1974.

Anthony Smart

Born in 1949 in Yorkshire. Studied at Hull College of Art, 1967–71, St Martin's School of Art, 1971–73. Working at Stockwell Depot and teaching at St Martin's School of Art and Brighton School of Art.

Group exhibitions include: 'Platform '72', Museum of Modern Art, Oxford, 1972; 'Six Sculptors', Chelsea Gallery, London, 1974; 'New Sculpture', Stockwell Depot, 1974; Group show, Norwich Cathedral Cloisters, 1975.

Michael Steiner

Born in 1945 in New York. One-man exhibitions at Fischbach Gallery, N.Y., 1962; Dwan Gallery, N.Y., 1966, 1968; Norman Mackenzie Art Gallery, University of Saskatchewan, Regina, 1970; Marlborough Gallery, N.Y., 1970, 1972, 1974; Makler Gallery, Philadelphia, 1970; David Mirvish Gallery, Toronto, 1970; Hart House, University of Toronto, 1971; Noah Goldowsky/Richard Bellamy, N.Y., 1972; Museum of Fine Arts, Boston, 1974. Group exhibitions include: 'Minimal Art', Gemeentemuseum, The Hague, 1968; 'The De Luxe Show', Houston, 1971; '11 Americans', Museum of Contemporary Art, Montreal, 1973–74.

Sylvia Stone

Born in 1928 in Toronto, Canada. Exhibited with Ronald Bladen at Brata Gallery, N.Y., 1959. One-woman exhibitions at the Tibor de Nagy Gallery, N.Y., 1967–69 and at the André Emmerich Gallery, N.Y., 1972, 1975. Group exhibitions include: 'Plastics and the New Art', Museum of Contemporary Art, Philadelphia, 1968 and 'Plastic Presence', Jewish Museum, N.Y., Milwaukee Art Center and San Francisco Museum, 1969.

Mark di Suvero

Born in 1933 in Shanghai, China. Immigrated with family to California, 1941. Studied at the University of California, Berkeley and Santa Barbara and at California School of Fine Arts. Moved to New York in 1957. First one-man exhibition at Green Gallery, 1960. Helped found Park Place Gallery (exhibition in 1966). Moved to Venice in protest of American involvement in Vietnam, 1971. One-man exhibitions include: Van Abbe Museum, Eindhoven and Wilhelm Lehmbruck Museum, Duisburg, 1972; 'Sculpture en Liberté', Saone.et Chalon, France, 1972; Drawings, Noah Goldowsky Gallery, N.Y., 1973; Richard Bellamy, N.Y., and Hansen Fuller Gallery, San Francisco, 1973; Whitney Museum of American Art, N.Y., 1975.

Brian Thompson

Born in 1950 in Morley, Yorkshire. Studying in the Department of Fine Art, Newcastle University, presently candidate for a M.F.A. degree.

Group exhibitions include: 'Northern Young Contemporaries', Whitworth Art Gallery, Manchester, 1973; Peter Stuyvesant Northern Painters and Sculptors Exhibition, Sunderland Arts Centre, 1974; Northern Arts Gallery, Newcastle-upon-Tyne, 1974; 'British Sculptors: Attitudes to Drawing', Sunderland Arts Centre, 1974.

William Tucker

Born in 1935 in Cairo. Studied sculpture at Central School of Art and Design and St Martin's School of Art, 1959–60. Recent exhibitions: XXXVI Venice Biennale, 1972; Serpentine Gallery, Arts Council, London, 1973.

David van de Kop

Born in 1937 in The Hague, Holland. Studied at the Royal Academy of Arts, The Hague and the Academy of Arts, Warsaw. Presently teaching at the Royal Academy of Arts, 's-Hertogenbosch, Holland. Work has been exhibited at the Stedelijk Museum, Amsterdam; Gemeentemuseum, The Hague; Gallery Espace, Amsterdam; Gallery Nouvelle Images, The Hague and at the Kröller-Müller National Museum, Otterlo in 1974. Sculpture commissioned by the Audio-Video Schakelcentrum, P.T.T.; Hilversum, Recreation Centre Rotte Meren and new office, S.U., of the Amsterdam subway.

Roger Williams

Born in 1943 in Dayton, Ohio. Studied at Cornell University, Ithaca, N.Y. (architecture); Hunter College, 1966–67. One-man exhibitions at Bennington College, Vermont, 1972; Usdan Gallery, Bennington, Vermont, 1973; Janie C. Lee Gallery, Houston, Texas, 1974; André Emmerich Gallery, N.Y., 1974. Group exhibitions include: André Emmerich Gallery, 1972; David Gallery, Rochester, N.Y.; Allen Center Competition, Houston, Texas, 1973.

Christopher Wilmarth

Born in 1943 in Sonoma, California. Studied at Cooper Union, N.Y., 1960–62, 1963–65. Presently teaching at Cooper Union. Awarded National Endowment for the Arts Grant, 1969 and Guggenheim

Fellowship, 1970. Awarded Commission for City University of New York, Mathematics Building, Mural Competition, 1974.

One-man exhibitions at Graham Gallery, N.Y., 1968; Paula Cooper Gallery, N.Y., 1971, 1972; Janie C. Lee Gallery, Dallas, 1971; Galleria dell'Ariete, Milan, 1973; Rosa Esman Gallery, N.Y., 1974; Daniel Weinberg Gallery, San Francisco, 1974; 'Nine Clearings for a Standing Man', Wadsworth Atheneum, Hartford, Conn., November 1974–January 1975 and St Louis Art Museum, 1975.

Jacqueline Winsor

Born in 1941 in Newfoundland, Canada. Studied at Yale Summer School of Art and Music, 1964; Massachusetts College of Art, 1965; Rutgers University, M.F.A., 1967. One-woman exhibitions at Douglass College Gallery, New Brunswick, New Jersey, 1968; Nova Scotia College of Art and Design, Halifax, N.S., 1971; Paula Cooper Gallery, N.Y., 1973. Group exhibitions include: 'Twenty-six by Twenty-six', Vassar College Art Gallery, Poughkeepsie, N.Y., 1971; 'Soft Sculpture', American Federation of Artists (travelling exhibition) 1968; 'Soft as Art', New York Cultural Center, N.Y., 1973; 'Four Young Americans', Allen Memorial Art Museum, Oberlin College, Oberlin, Ohio, 1974; '8th Biennial of Paris', Musée d'Arte Moderne, Paris, 1973; 'Painting & Sculpture Today; 1974', Indianapolis Museum of Art and Contemporary Art Center, Cincinnati, Ohio, 1974.

Isaac Witkin

Born in 1938 in Johannesburg, South Africa. Moved to England in 1956. Studied at St. Martin's School of Art, 1957–60. Assistant to Henry Moore, 1961–63. Taught at Maidstone College of Art, Kent, St. Martin's School of Art and Ravensbourne School of Art, Kent. 1965– Artist-in-Residence, Bennington College, Vermont.

One-man exhibitions at Rowan Gallery, London, 1963; Robert Elkon Gallery, N.Y., 1965–1973; Waddington Galleries, London, 1966, 1968; University of Bridgeport, Conn., 1970; Robert Hull Fleming Museum, University of Vermont, Burlington, 1971; Marlborough Gallery, N.Y., 1975. Group exhibitions include: 'The New Generation: 1965', Whitechapel Art Gallery, London, 1965; 'Primary Structures', Jewish Museum, N.Y., 1965; 'British Sculpture of the Sixties', London, 1970.

James Wolfe

Born in 1944 in New York. Studied at Solebury School. Technical Director, Theater Department and Technical Assistant, Sculpture Department, Bennington College, Vermont. One-man exhibitions at the André Emmerich Gallery, N.Y., 1973, 1974. Group exhibitions include: The Deluxe Show, Houston, Texas, 1972; 'Contemporary Sculpture', The Phillips Collection, Washington, D.C., 1972; 'New England Sculpture' at Dartmouth College, Hanover, New Hampshire and tour; 'Contemporary American Artists', Cleveland Museum of Art, Ohio, 1973/74.

Photographic credits

Walter Russell, N.Y.	Andre *a*
John Weber Gallery	Andre *b*
Heini Schneebeli	Bates *a, b, c, d*
Felicity Samuel Gallery	Bell *a, b, c*
Joel Greenberg	Bolus *a, b*
Royal Academy	Evans *a*
Eileen Tweedy	Evans *b, c*
Jonathan Bayer	Hall *a, b, c*
David Scribner	Hatcher *a, c*
Lynton Money	Hawkes *a, c*
Schopplein Studio, San Francisco	Hudson *a, b, c*
Rowan Gallery	King *c*
Leicester Galleries	Lowe *a, b*
Loren Madsen	Madsen *a*
Steve Kahn	Madsen *b, d*
Los Angeles County Museum of Art	Madsen *c*
Geoffrey Clements, N.Y.	Murray *c, d*
Robert Murray	Murray *a, b*
Sue Wells	Nash *a, b*
Ian Todd	Neagu *c, d*
Tibor de Nagy Gallery, N.Y.	Reginato *c*
Pace Gallery, N.Y.	Samaras *a, b, c, d, e*
Museum of Fine Arts, Boston	Scott *b*
Leo Castelli Gallery	Serra *c, d*
Lois Steen	Steiner *a*
Robert E. Mates and Paul Katz	Steiner *b, c*
Bevan Davies, N.Y.	Stone *a*
Geoffrey Clements, N.Y.	Stone *b, c*
Richard Bellamy	di Suvero *a, b*
Sean Hudson	Tucker *b*
S. Waltzer	Williams *c*
Robert E. Mates and Paul Katz	Wilmarth *c*
Geoffrey Clements, N.Y.	Winsor *a, c*
Vermont Photographers Co-Op	Witkin *b, c, d*
Vermont Photographers Co-Op	Wolfe *a, b, c*